THE CAMBRIDGE ANCIENT HISTORY

SECOND VOLUME OF PLATES

Cambridge University Press
Fetter Lane, London

New York
Bombay, Calcutta, Madras
Toronto
Macmillan

Tokyo
Maruzen-Kabushiki-Kaisha

THE
CAMBRIDGE
ANCIENT HISTORY

EDITED BY

J. B. BURY, M.A., F.B.A.

S. A. COOK, Litt.D.

F. E. ADCOCK, M.A.

VOLUME OF PLATES II

PREPARED BY

C. T. SELTMAN, M.A.

CAMBRIDGE

AT THE UNIVERSITY PRESS

1928

PRINTED IN GREAT BRITAIN

PREFACE

In the first volume of plates illustrations were given of the handi-
work of those peoples whose history was written in the first four
volumes of the *Cambridge Ancient History*. The purpose of the
present book is to provide illustrations for vols. v and vi of that
work, which treat of the Mediterranean world of which Greece was
the centre during the fifth and fourth centuries B.C. This explains
the fact that the major part of this volume is devoted to examples
of Greek sculpture, painting and architecture of those centuries;
but since the chapter on Greek Art in vol. v treats of late archaic,
as well as of classical Greek art, works of the closing decades of
the sixth century are also given. Besides these will be found
illustrations of coins which are cited in the text as possessing
evidential importance for history and some specimens of Egyptian
work selected to make clear certain points in vol. vi, chap. vi.

Thus the purpose of this volume is ancillary, and consideration
of this has governed the selection of subjects for illustration. For
this in Greek sculpture and painting the volume is indebted to
Professor Beazley, in Greek architecture to Mr D. S. Robertson,
in Egyptian Art to Dr H. R. Hall. The writers of the various
historical chapters have been consulted about the choice of the coins.
The responsibility for the limitation of plates, which is due to the
desire to keep the volume within certain bounds of price, does not,
however, rest with the contributors to vols. v and vi. The commentaries on the plates illustrating art and architecture are due to
the several contributors[1]; for the commentary on the coins and
Greek fortifications the present writer is responsible.

It is hoped that this volume will be of assistance to readers of
vols. v and vi; at the same time the volume itself has, within its
limits, an interest of its own. For the reader may gain an idea of the
progress of Greek sculpture, painting and architecture, and in the
plates of coins he will find not only evidence for political history but
evidence of art as well. Moreover, the few Egyptian antiquities of

[1] For the commentaries on pp. 18 to 70 and 80 to 110, Professor Beazley;
for pp. 72 to 78 and 112 to 116, Mr D. S. Robertson; for pp. 14, 16, 118, 120,
Dr H. R. Hall.

v

Saïte and early Ptolemaic times both serve their immediate purpose of illustrating the text and show something of the later phases of Egyptian art.

Grateful acknowledgments are due to the Society for the Promotion of Hellenic Studies for the loan of photographs, and to Mrs Beazley, Mr Ashmole, Dr K. Neugebauer, Mr L. P. Thompson and Mr M. Ziffo for supplying photographs in their possession, as well as to the Director of the British Museum for permission to reproduce numerous pictures, including that of the recently acquired decadrachm depicting Alexander pursuing the elephant of Porus, to Professors R. Zahn and Valentin Müller for prints from the Antiquarium and the University in Berlin, to Dr Caskey, Miss G. M. A. Richter and Professor B. Schröder for prints from the Boston Museum of Fine Arts, the Metropolitan Museum of Art in New York and the Albertinum in Dresden. The Preussische Akademie der Wissenschaften and the Deutsches Archaeologisches Institut have again generously sanctioned the reproduction of various pictures. For the provision of plaster casts of coins thanks are due to Dr G. F. Hill, Keeper of Coins and Medals in the British Museum, to Professor K. Regling, Monsieur J. Babelon and Monsieur V. Tourneur of the Cabinets of Coins in Berlin, in the Bibliothèque Nationale, Paris, and in Brussels, and also to Monsieur R. Jameson.

The following publishers have kindly sanctioned the reproduction of pictures from the books specified:

E. Boccard, Paris (*Les Fouilles de Delphes*).
F. Bruckmann A.G., Munich (Furtwängler and Reichhold, *Griech. Vasenmalerei*; Brunn's *Denkmäler*; Riezler,*Weissgrundige attische Lekythen*).
G. D. W. Callwey, Munich (*Münchener Jahrbuch der Bildenden Kunst*).
N. G. Elwertsche Buchhandlung, Marburg (Bieber, *Die Antike Skulpturen d. kgl. Museum in Cassel*).
P. Geuthner, Paris (Dugas, *Le Sanctuaire d'Aléa Athéna à Tegéa au IVᵉ siècle*).
W. de Gruyter and Co., Berlin (Wiegand and Schrader, *Priene*).
Hölder, Pichler, Tempsky A.G., Vienna (Schrader, *Auswahl arch. Marmor-Skulpturen im Akropolis Museum*).
Kunstgeschichtliches Seminar der Universität, Marburg (Buschor and Hamann, *Die Skulpt. des Zeustempels in Olympia*).
E. Leroux, Paris (Hamdy Bey and Reinach, *Une Nécropole Royale à Sidon*).
J. Springer, Berlin (*Olympia, Ergebnisse der Ausgrabungen*).

PREFACE

The care and accuracy of the Staff of the University Press is again deserving of grateful acknowledgment.

The design on the outside cover represents a bronze statuette of a hoplite, wearing a crested Corinthian helmet, a cuirass and greaves, and carrying a shield of Boeotian shape. This figurine, found at Dodona and now in Berlin, is of the early fifth century B.C.

C. T. S.

June 1928

TABLE OF CONTENTS

ix

CONTENTS

CONTENTS

xi

CONTENTS

[a], [b], [c] Gold coins of *Syracuse, Gela* and *Acragas* issued probably under pressure from the Carthaginian invasion 410–406 B.C.
[a] ΣΥΡΑ. Head of Heracles. Rev. ΣΥΡΑ. Head of Arethusa.
[b] ΓΕΛΑΣ. Protome of river-bull. Rev. ΣΩΣΙΓΟΛΙΣ. Head of
goddess. [c] ΑΚΡΑ. Eagle. Rev. ΣΙΛΑΝΟΣ (magistrate). Crab.
Formerly *Pozzi Coll.* 603, 444, 385. Wts. [a] 1·15 g.; [b] 1·13 g.;
[c] 1·32 g. (v, 22.)
The *Carthaginian* invasion produced the first Punic coinage.
[d] Tetradrachm minted in Sicily 410–406 B.C. Nike over horse.
Rev. Date-palm (Punic inscr.) 'The Camp.' *Brit. Mus.* Wt.
16·85 g. (v, 23.)
[e], [f], [g] The principal currency of the Greeks in Asia Minor
was of electrum: typical are staters of *Cyzicus, Mitylene* and
Lampsacus which retain as reverse the archaic type of quartered
incuse square. [e] Tunny fish (the city device), over it Delphic
omphalos between eagles. Formerly *Sir H. Weber Coll.* 5024.
Wt. 16·03 g. [f] ΜΥΤΙ. Head of Apollo. *B. M. C. Troas, etc.*,
p. 158, 28. Wt. 15·45 g. [g] Protome of Pegasus in vine-wreath.
B. M. C. Mysia, p. 79, 8. Wt. 15·26 g. (v, 23; vi, 59.)
[h] *Themistocles* as ruler of *Magnesia*. About 463–450 B.C. Didrachm of Attic weight. ΘΕΜΙΣ[ΤΟΚΛΕ]ΟΣ. Apollo with bay-
laurel branch and falcon. Rev. ΜΑ. Falcon. *Berlin Mus.* Wt.
8·59 g. (v, 64.)
[i] *Rhodes.* Tetradrachm of Attic weight. About 407 B.C. Head of
Helios. Rev. ΡΟΔΙΟΝ. Rose and two bunches of grapes. *Bibl.
Nat. Paris.* Wt. 16·92 g. (v, 23, 355.)
Between 478 and 457 B.C. certain Boeotian cities, repudiating
Theban supremacy, issued autonomous coins with a Boeotian shield
as obverse type.
[j], [k] [j] *Haliartus.* Stater. Rev. ΑᑭΙ (Ariartus). Amphora.
[k] *Tanagra.* Stater. Rev. ΤΑ. Protome of horse. *B. M. C. Central
Greece*, p. 49, 11; p. 61, 23. Wts. 12·21 g.; 11·89 g. (v, 79.)
[l] *Himera.* Under the rule of *Theron* and *Thrasydaeus* of Acragas.
About 482–472 B.C. Didrachm. ΗΙΜΕΡΑ. Cock. Rev. Crab (device of Acragas). Formerly *Pozzi Coll.* 453. Wt. 8·5 g. (v, 146.)
[m] *Syracuse* under *Hiero.* Tetradrachm struck shortly after his
naval victory over the Etruscans in 474 B.C. Victorious Chariot;
beneath, a sea monster. Rev. Head of Arethusa and dolphins (cf.
the 'Demareteion' struck in 480 B.C., *Vol. of Plates*, i, 308 [g]).
Formerly *Pozzi Coll.* 573. Wt. 17·08 g. (v, 148.)
[n] *Aetna.* Founded by Hiero in 475 B.C. on the site of Catana.
Tetradrachm. ΑΙΤΝΑΙΟΝ. Head of Silenus, scarabaeus below.
Rev. Zeus enthroned, pine tree and eagle. *Brussels Mus.* Wt.
17·24 g. (v, 147.)
[o] *Catana* restored in 461 B.C. Tetradrachm. Chariot. Rev.
ΚΑΤΑΝΑΙΟΝ. Head of Apollo. Formerly *Pozzi Coll.* 410. Wt.
17·21 g. (v, 155.)

[a]   [d]   [c]

[b]

[e]   [.f]   [g]   [h]

[i]   [j]   [k]   [l]

[m]   [n]   [o]

[*a*] Tetradrachm probably minted by the *Athenian Fleet* in *Samos* in 411 B.C. To the customary Athenian type is added a small bull's head (a city device of Samos). *Bibl. Nat. Paris.* Wt. 16·50 g. (v, 333.)

[*b*], [*c*] *New Sybaris.* Founded in 445 B.C. Tetrobol. *Thurii* founded in 443 B.C. Stater. The obverse type of both is Athenian; the bull on the reverse having been the type of old Sybaris (cf. *Vol. of Plates*, i, 306 [*f*]). [*b*] *Bibl. Nat. Paris.* Wt. 2·38 g. [*c*] Formerly *Pozzi Coll.* 226. Wt. 7·7 g. (v, 168.)

[*d*] *Athens.* Gold drachma, 407–406 B.C. For this coinage golden statues of Victory were melted before the battle of Arginusae. *Berlin Mus.* Wt. 4·3 g. (v, 22, 355.)

[*e*] *Athens.* Copper tetradrachm thinly washed with silver, first issued in 406 B.C. after the treasury was exhausted. This money of necessity was demonetized in 393 B.C. (cf. Aristophanes, *Frogs*, 717–732; *Eccles.* 816–822). *Bibl. Nat. Paris.* Wt. 18 g. (v, 355; vi, 35.)

[*f*], [*g*], [*h*] Three coins struck during the Satraps' revolt against Persia. [*f*] *Datames, Satrap of Cappadocia.* Persic drachm, about 372–366 B.C., struck at *Sinope* with the types of that city. Head of nymph. Rev. Sea-eagle on dolphin; beneath, **ΔΑΤΑΜΑ**. *Brit. Mus.* Wt. 5·89 g. (vi, 20.) [*g*] *Orontes, Satrap of Dascylium.* Gold stater issued about 362 B.C. in *Lampsacus.* Idealized portrait of the Satrap. Rev. Protome of Pegasus. *Bibl. Nat. Paris.* Wt. 8·43 g. (vi, 21.)

[*h*] Gold stater issued by *Tachos* (or *Taos*), *King of Egypt*, who, with Athenian aid, supported the Satraps in revolt. About 366–359 B.C. The weight is that of a Persian daric, the types Athenian, the legend, **TAO**. *Brit. Mus.* Wt. 8·3 g. (vi, 21.)

[*i*] Gold coin of daric weight, probably minted by *Thibron* at *Ephesus* as pay for the remnant of 'the Ten Thousand,' in 399 B.C. Obv. Bee. Rev. Quartered incuse square. *Jameson Coll.* Wt. 8·29 g. (vi, 38.)

[*j*] *Thebes.* Quarter stater of pale gold issued in 394 B.C., possibly from Persian subsidies. Head of Dionysus. Rev. Infant Heracles strangling serpents. *Jameson Coll.* Wt. 3·02 g. (vi, 49.)

[*k*]–[*p*] The silver coinage of a *Maritime League* founded shortly after Conon's victory over the Spartans off Cnidus in 394 B.C. **ΣΥΝ**(μαχικόν) appears on all the coins, and pro-Theban sympathies induced the common obverse type of Heracles strangling serpents, while each state placed on the reverse its own city device.

[*k*] *Rhodes.* Rose. [*l*] *Cnidus.* Head of Aphrodite and prow. [*m*] *Samos.* Lion's scalp. [*n*] *Iasus.* Head of Apollo. [*o*] *Ephesus.* Bee. [*p*] *Byzantium.* Bull on dolphin. The *British Museum* has recently acquired a coin of a seventh member of this League, hitherto unknown, *Cyzicus.* Tunny fish and lion's head (*Brit. Mus. Quarterly*, ii, p. 59, Pl. XXXV, 1). [*k*], [*p*] *Boston Mus., Warren Coll.* Wts. 11·35 g.; 11·29 g. [*l*]–[*o*] *Berlin Mus.* Wts. 11·35 g.; 11·02 g.; 10·73 g.; 10·76 g. (vi, 50.)

[a]   [b]   [c]   [d]   [e]

[f]   [g]   [h]   [i]   [j]

[k]   [l]

[m]   [n]

[o]   [p]

[a], [b], [c] Autonomous silver coins of Boeotian cities issued 381–379 B.C. during the eclipse of Theban power, cf. p. 2 [j], [k]. All have a Boeotian shield as obverse type. [a] *Thespiae*. Head of Aphrodite Melainis and two crescents. [b] *Plataea*. Head of Hera. [c] *Orchomenus*. **EPXO**. Amphora. [a], [b] *Bibl. Nat. Paris*. Wts. 12·4 g.; 2·76 g. [c] *B. M. C. Central Greece*, p. 54, 22. Wt. 12 g. (vi, 64.)

[d] The *Arcadians* at *Olympia*. Gold coinage minted from the sacred treasures, ostensibly in the name of the Pisatans in 364 B.C., though the types—Zeus and thunderbolt—are those of Elean issues at Olympia. **ΠΙΣΑ** beside the thunderbolt fixes responsibility on the Eleans' rivals. *B. M. C. Pelop.*, p. 76, 1. Wt. 1·04 g. (vi, 98.)

[e] *Alexander of Pherae*, as Tagus of Thessaly, 369–357 B.C. Stater. Head of Hecate. Rev. Horseman; beneath, double axe. *B. M. C. Thessaly*, p. 47, 14. Wt. 11·86 g. (vi, 84.)

[f] *Federal coinage* struck as pay for the mercenaries of the *Arcadian League*, founded about 370 B.C. Silver stater with the head of Zeus, and Pan seated on a mountain-top, types which were later continued on the coins of Megalopolis, the new capital of this League. *B. M. C. Pelop.*, p. 173, 48. Wt. 12·34 g. (vi, 88.)

[g] The *Achaean League* first issued a Federal coinage about 366 B.C., the principal unit being a stater with the head of Artemis Laphria and the figure of Zeus Amarius. *Brit. Mus.* Wt. 12 g. (vi, 95.)

[h] *Carthaginian* tetradrachm minted at *Panormus* shortly after 400 B.C., the types being copied from Syracusan models. Under the chariot appears the enigmatic Punic legend 'Ziz.' *B. M. C. Italy*, p. 247, 10. Wt. 17·43 g. (vi, 109.)

[i] Himera after its destruction by the Carthaginians was re-founded as *Thermae*, a Punic settlement to which Greeks migrated. Its tetradrachms, Punic in character, are at first anepigraphic but later bear the Greek legend **ΘΕΡΜΙΤΑΝ**. *Bibl. Nat. Paris*. Wt. 17·3 g. (vi, 110.)

[j] *Issa*, off the Dalmatian coast, as a Syracusan colony of Dionysius I. A bronze coin of Sicilian fabric with the head of the hero **ΙΟΝΙΟΣ** and a dolphin. *Glasgow, Hunter Coll.* (vi, 129 sq.)

[k] *Catana* and *Leontini* about 403 B.C. formed a defensive alliance against Dionysius I, which is attested by this hemidrachm, with **ΛΕΟΝ**, head of Apollo and **ΚΑΤΑΝΑΙΟΝ**, river-bull and fish. *Jameson Coll.* Wt. 1·93 g. (vi, 119.)

[l]–[p] Coinage of *Philip of Macedon*. Before 356 B.C. Thasian settlers on this mainland, at the mining town of *Crenides*, issued gold staters [l] with the head of Heracles and a tripod, inscribed **ΘΑΣΙΟΝ ΗΠΕΙΡΟ**. After Philip annexed this settlement in 356 B.C., and re-named it *Philippi*, a few gold coins appeared [m] with identical types, but with legend **ΦΙΛΙΠΠΩΝ**. These were quickly superseded by the royal Macedonian coinage, [n], [o] a half-stater and stater with the inscription **ΦΙΛΙΠΠΟΥ**. The latter coin obtained a world-wide reputation and was imitated from the Danube to Northumbria. [p] A silver tetradrachm struck contemporaneously with the last coins, the reverse type of which, a victorious racehorse, refers to Philip's victory at Olympia in 356 B.C. [m] *B. M. C. Macedonia*, p. 96, 1. Wt. 8·62 g. [l], [n]–[p] *Bibl. Nat. Paris*. Wts. —; 4·3 g.; 8·6 g.; 14·48 g. (vi, 208, 209.)

[a]　　[b]　　[c]　　[d]　　[e]

[f]　　[g]　　[h]　　[i]

[j]　　[k]　　[j]

[l]　　[m]　　[n]　　[o]　　[p]

[a] *Mausolus, Dynast of Caria*, obtained possession of the island of Cos, 355 B.C. To this period belongs a Coan tetradrachm with head of Heracles whose features resemble those of the prince. The crab is the civic device. *B. M. C. Caria*, p. 195, 11. Wt. 14·3 g. (vi, 212.)

[b], [c] Bronze coinage of the *Sacred War* minted in *Phocis* by *Onomarchus* and his successor *Phalaecus*, 356–346 B.C. The bull's head on each is the Phocian device and **ONYMAPXOY** and **ΦΑΛΑΙΚΟΥ** appear within the wreaths. [b] *B. M. C. Central Greece*, p. 23, 104. [c] *Sir H. Weber Coll.* 3184. (vi, 216.)

[d] The *Amphictyonic Council* issued in the spring of 338 B.C. silver staters in its own name. The head of Demeter of Anthela, the figure of Pythian Apollo and the inscription **ΑΜΦΙΚΤΙΟΝΩΝ** appear on the coins. *B. M. C. Central Greece*, p. 27, 22. Wt. 12·14 g. (vi, 260.)

[e]–[h] *Timoleon in Sicily*, 343–337 B.C. [f] The Syracusan silver coinage of Timoleon resembles [e] the contemporary Corinthian coinage, but the former bears the Syracusan ethnic. Some of his bronze coins [g] have a bearded head, identified as Archias, the first Corinthian founder of Syracuse. Acragas, after Timoleon's re-settlement, renewed its coinage [h], combining the free horse, a Syracusan type, with a crab, the original city's device. [e], [f] *B. M. C. Corinth, etc.*, p. 47, 390; p. 98, 3. Wts. 8·21 g.; 8·66 g. [g] *Giesecke Coll.* [h] *B. M. C. Sicily*, p. 13, 75. Wt. 2·1 g. (vi, 293, 298.)

[i]–[k] [i] Silver stater of *Alexander, son of Neoptolemus*, King of Epirus, struck probably at Tarentum 334–332 B.C.; contemporary with this is a bronze coin [j] of Syracuse, with head of Zeus, thunderbolt and eagle as on the Tarentine piece. Locri in South Italy issued at the same time a silver stater [k] with kindred types. This similarity of types may indicate an alliance. [i] *B. M. C. Thessaly, etc.*, p. 110, 3. Wt. 10·71 g. [j] *Berlin Mus.* [k] *B. M. C. Italy*, p. 364, 6. Wt. 7·65 g. (vi, 301.)

[l]–[o] *Alexander the Great.* [l] The king's portrait on a tetradrachm of Lysimachus struck in 300 B.C. [m], [o] Gold staters of Alexander's Imperial coinage, the first minted in Macedon with the serpent on Athena's helmet and the name **ΑΛΕΞΑΝΔΡΟΥ** behind Nike; the second minted in the East with the Persian lion-gryphon on the helmet and the title **ΒΑΣΙΛΕΩΣ** added. [n] A silver tetradrachm minted in Macedon. [l], [m] *Seltman Coll.* Wts. 16·29 g.; 8·6 g. [n] Formerly *Pozzi Coll.* Wt. 17·17 g. [o] *Bibl. Nat. Paris.* Wt. 8·58 g. (vi, 155, 387, 427.)

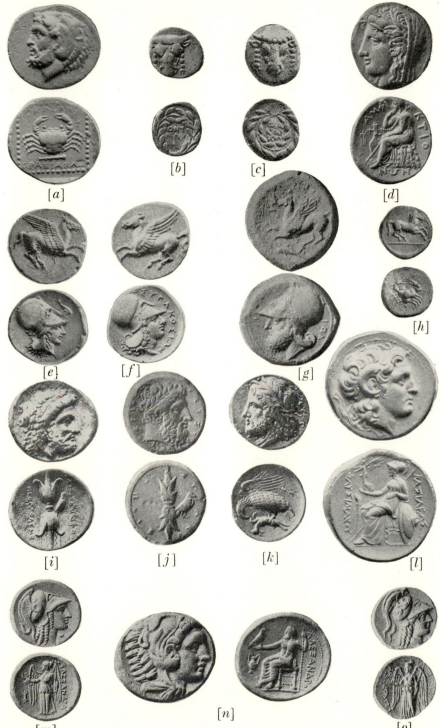

[a]

[b]

[c]

[d]

[e]

[f]

[g]

[h]

[i]

[j]

[k]

[l]

[m]

[n]

[o]

[a] Decadrachm struck, perhaps in Babylon, shortly after Alexander's death, depicting him on horseback pursuing the elephant of the Indian King Porus. On the reverse is a figure of Alexander holding a thunderbolt. *Brit. Mus. Quarterly*, i, p. 36. Wt. 39·62 g. (vi, 409.)

[b] Tetradrachm of *Seleucus I*. The elephant, the anchor, and the head of the horned horse Bucephalus, all badges of the Seleucid dynasty, appear on this coin. Seleucus set especial store by elephants as a weapon in war and bartered whole provinces to obtain them. *Berlin Mus.* Wt. 16·59 g. (vi, 409.)

[c] *Agathocles, King of Bactria and North-West India*, about 150 B.C. issued a series of tetradrachms commemorating his predecessors and bearing the coin-types which each of them had once employed. On this series, Diodotus and Euthydemus are designated gods, Alexander is merely 'Son of Philip.' In Central Asia he was not 'divine.' *B. M. C. India, Greek and Scythic Kings*, p. 10, 1. Wt. 16·28 g. (vi, 433.)

[d] Tetradrachm minted by *Archon, Satrap of Babylon*, about 322 B.C. The issue of this and other Satrapal coins, after Alexander's death, indicates the increased authority of the local governors. *B. M. C. Arabia, etc.*, p. 185, 22. Wt. 16·94 g. (vi, 465.)

[e] *Cassander, King of Macedon*, claiming to be the successor of the Macedonian Philip, revived on his bronze coinage the types employed by Alexander's father, the head of Heracles and the victorious race-horse (cf. p. 6 [n], [p] above). *Seltman Coll.* (vi, 482.)

[f] Cassander's crazy brother *Alexarchus* refounded Sane on the peninsula of Acte as *Uranopolis* and issued fanciful coins for his 'children of heaven.' On the obverse of the tetradrachm is Aphrodite Urania seated on the globe and the legend **ΟΥΡΑΝΙΔΩΝ**; on the reverse are the sun, moon and five planets. *Berlin Mus. Cat. Macedon*, p. 162, 1. Wt. 13·5 g. (vi, 482.)

[g]–[j] The gradual breaking up of Alexander's Empire is reflected in the Alexander coinage, which was at first continued unaltered by most of his successors, but on which other names besides that of the dead king presently began to appear. [g] *Aspeisas, Satrap of Susiana*, put his name in the field of a tetradrachm, about 316–312 B.C. (vi, 488.) [h] *Nicocles, King of Paphos* in Cyprus, issued Alexander tetradrachms before 309 B.C. with his own name on the mane of Heracles' lion's scalp. (vi, 494.) By 300 B.C. *Demetrius the Besieger* was issuing gold staters [j] with Alexander's types but with the legend **ΔΗΜΗΤΡΙΟΥ ΒΑΣΙΛΕΩΣ**. E. T. Newell, *The Coinages of Demetrius Poliorcetes*, 1927, p. 14, note 1, adduces good grounds for supposing that the similar stater [i] with the name of Antigonus is probably to be referred to the son rather than to the father of Demetrius. (vi, 502.) [g] *Brit. Mus.* Wt. 16·94 g. [h] Formerly *Yakountchikoff Coll.* [i], [j] *Brit. Mus.* Wts. 8·6 g.; 8·55 g.

[k] Demetrius celebrated his victory off Salamis in Cyprus by the issue of tetradrachms minted at Salamis about 300 B.C. On the obverse is Victory upon the prow of a captured vessel, on the reverse Poseidon and the king's name and title. *Brit. Mus.* Wt. 17·24 g. (vi, 499.)

[a]

[b]

[c]

[d]

[e]

[f]

[g]

[h]

[i]

[j]

[k]

FORTIFICATIONS

[a] THE WALLS OF MESSENE built by Epaminondas in 370–369 B.C. furnish one of the best extant specimens of Greek military architecture, being built of finely wrought ashlar masonry. Beyond the figure in the picture are the remains of one of the gates, and the wall itself vanishes in the distance where it climbs the hillside. (vi, 90.)

[*Phot. Hellenic Society*]

[b] EURYALUS, the castle of Dionysius I above Syracuse. The photograph shows the remains of rooms and a wide passage that was once underground. Walls ran from this castle to the city and the fortification made Syracuse the strongest of all Greek cities. (vi, 119.)

[*Phot. Alinari*]

[a] THE WALLS OF MESSENE

[b] EURYALUS

[a] Portrait profile of PSAMMETICHUS I, from an intercolumnar slab in the *British Museum* (no. 20). Shows the influence of the Saïte-Theban school of portrait sculpture (see *Vol. of Plates*, i, 268). XXVIIth Dynasty; about 620 B.C. (Repeated to show the style from vol. i, p. 270 [b].)

[b] Similar profile, also from an intercolumnar slab of king NAKHTENĒBEF (NECTANEBO I), 378–361 B.C. XXXth Dynasty. *Brit. Mus.* no. 22. (vi, 159.)

[c], [d] PORTRAIT-HEADS OF KINGS: sculptor's models; of the XXXth Dynasty or early Ptolemaic period. Good examples. *Brit. Mus.* nos. 14392, 13316; (c) height 14 cm., (d) height 10·5 cm. (vi, 160.)

[a]

[b]

[c]

[d]

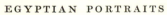

EGYPTIAN PORTRAITS

Part of the so-called METTERNICH STELE, now in the *Castle of Königswart* near *Marienbad*. This is probably the best known of a type of magical stele, very common in small sizes, which well illustrates the superstitions of the religion of later days in Egypt, with its prayers, its figures of prophylactic snakes and crocodiles, etc. The idea of it is of course the victory of good, personified by the child Horus, over evil, in the next world. Fourth century B.C. (vi, 164.)

[W. Golenisheff, *die Metternichstele*, Pl. I]

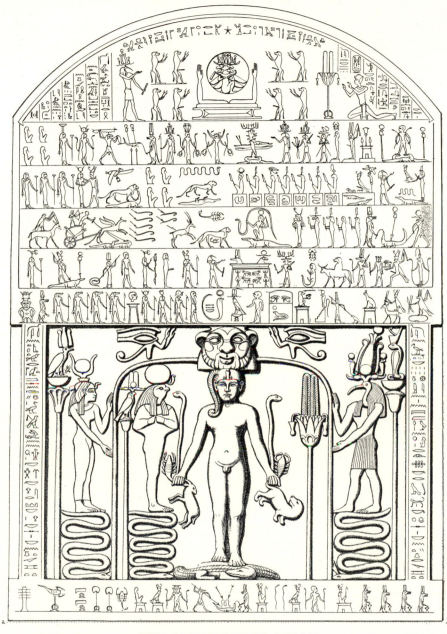

THE METTERNICH STELE

[a] Marble youth ('Kouros')—the so-called Strangford Apollo—from *Anaphe* (?); in the *British Museum*. About 490 B.C. (v, 420.)

[b] Marble woman ('Kore') from the *Acropolis of Athens*; in *Athens* (Acropolis no. 674). About 500 B.C. (v, 421.)

[H. Schrader, *Auswahl arch. Marmor. Sculpt. im Akrop. Mus.*, fig. 22]

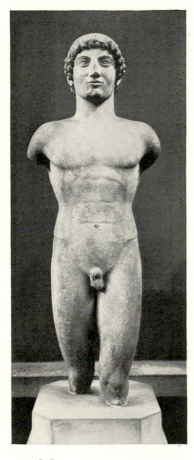

[a] YOUTH, FROM
ANAPHE (?)

[b] WOMAN, FROM THE
ACROPOLIS OF ATHENS

[a] Marble woman ('Kore') from the *Acropolis of Athens*; in *Athens* (Acropolis no. 684). About 500 B.C. (v, 421.)

[b] Marble woman ('Kore') dedicated by Euthydicus, from the *Acropolis of Athens*; in *Athens* (Acropolis nos. 686 and 609). About 490–480 B.C. (v, 421, 427.)

[H. Schrader, *l.c.*, Pl. 9, figs. 30, 31]

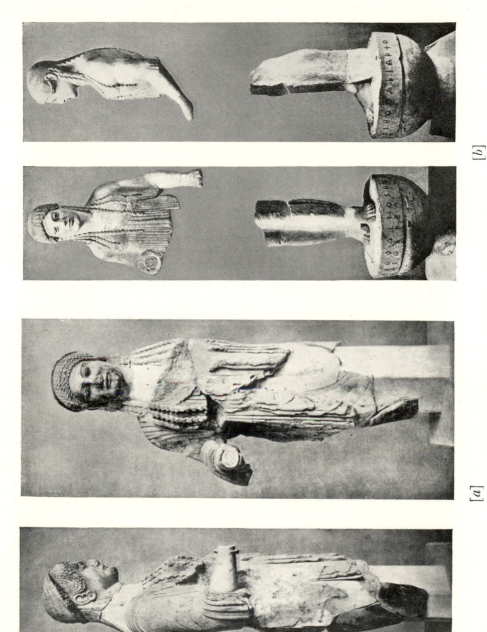

[a]

[b]

WOMEN, FROM THE ACROPOLIS

[*a*] One of the metopes of the Athenian Treasury at Delphi; in *Delphi*. Heracles and the Stag. End of the sixth century B.C. (iv, 597; v, 422.)

[*Phot. Alinari*]

[*b*] Athena slaying a Giant; in *Athens*. The central group of a marble gigantomachy which filled the Peisistratid pediment of the old Temple of Athena on the Acropolis at Athens. In the *Acropolis Museum*. About 520–510 B.C. (iv, 66; v, 421.)

[*Phot. F. Bruckmann A.G., Munich*]

[a] METOPE IN DELPHI

[b] GROUP FROM THE ACROPOLIS

[*a*], [*b*] Theseus carrying off the Queen of the Amazons; in *Chalcis*; from one of the pediments of the Temple of Apollo at *Eretria*. Marble. About 510 B.C. (v, 422.)

[From *Antike Denkmäler*]

[*c*] Heracles from the East Pediment of the Temple of Aphaia at *Aegina*; in *Munich*. Marble. Modern, the nose, the bow, the left lower leg, the right foot. About 490–480 B.C. (v, 422.)

[*Phot. F. Bruckmann A.G., Munich*]

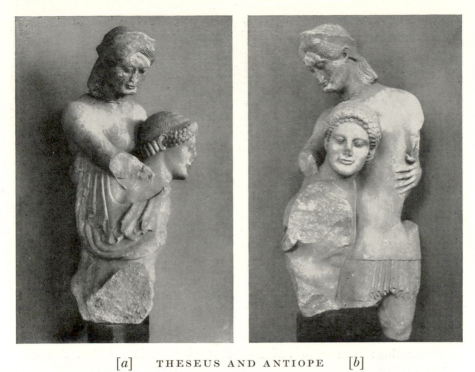

[a]   THESEUS AND ANTIOPE   [b]

[c] HERACLES

[*a*] Heracles and Antaeus: from a calyx-krater by Euphronius; in the *Louvre, Paris*. About 510 B.C. (v, 423, 425.)

[*Furtwängler and Reichhold*, Pl. 72; F. Bruckmann A.G., Munich]

[*b*] Arming: from an amphora by Euthymides; in *Munich*. About 510 B.C. (v, 424 *sq.*)

[*L.c.*, Pl. 81]

[a] FROM A KRATER BY EUPHRONIUS

[b] FROM AN AMPHORA BY EUTHYMIDES

[*a*] Amazons: from a drinking-cup by the Panaitius painter; in the *British Museum*. About 500 B.C. (v, 425.)

[*b*] Zeus carrying off a woman: from a drinking-cup by Duris; in the *Louvre, Paris*. About 490 B.C. (v, 425.)

[*Photograph by Mrs Beazley*]

[a] FROM A CUP BY THE PANAITIUS PAINTER

[b] FROM A CUP BY DURIS

LATE ARCHAIC PAINTING

[*a*] Dionysus and Silenus: from a drinking-cup by the Brygus painter; in the *Cabinet des Médailles, Paris*. About 490–480 B.C. (v, 425.)

[*Phot. Giraudon*]

[*b*] Menelaus and Helen: from a kotyle (drinking-bowl) by Macron; in *Boston*. About 490–480 B.C. (v, 425.)

[*Furtwängler and Reichhold*, Pl. 85; F. Bruckmann A.G., Munich]

30

[a] FROM A CUP BY THE BRYGUS PAINTER

[b] FROM A KOTYLE BY MACRON

[*a*] Hermes and a Silen: from an amphora by the Berlin painter; in *Berlin*. About 490 B.C. (v, 425.)

[*Furtwängler and Reichhold*, Pl. 134]

[*b*] Theseus wrestling with Cercyon: from a drinking-cup by the Cleophrades painter; in the *Cabinet des Médailles, Paris*. About 490 B.C. (v, 425.)

[*Photograph by Mrs Beazley*]

[*c*] Artemis and Actaeon: from a bell-krater by the Pan painter; in *Boston*. About 480–470 B.C. (v, 425.)

[*Furtwängler and Reichhold*, Pl. 115]

[a] FROM AN AMPHORA BY
THE BERLIN PAINTER

[b] FROM A CUP BY THE
CLEOPHRADES PAINTER

[c] FROM A KRATER BY THE PAN PAINTER

[*a*] Marble boy: from the Acropolis of Athens; in *Athens* (Acropolis no. 698). About 480 B.C. (v, 426.)

[H. Schrader, *Auswahl arch. Marmor. Sculpt. im Akrop. Mus.*, Pl. 16]

[*b*], [*c*] Head of a boy (fragment of a marble statue): from the Acropolis of Athens; in *Athens* (Acropolis no. 689). About 480 B.C. (v, 427.)

[*Photographs by Professor Jacobsthal*]

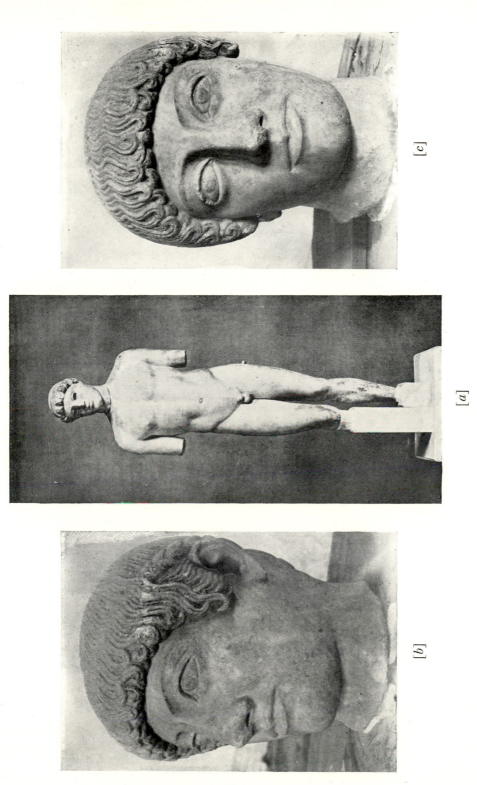

[c]

[a]

[b]

SCULPTURE FROM THE ACROPOLIS OF ATHENS

3-2

[*a*] Bronze charioteer: from Delphi; in *Delphi*. Part of a chariot-group dedicated by the Syracusan Polyzelus about 470 B.C. (v, 427.)

[*Fouilles de Delphes*, iv, Pl. 50]

[*b*] Marble Apollo: from the west pediment of the Temple of Zeus at Olympia; in *Olympia*. About 460 B.C. (v, 427, 430.) Cf. below pp. 44, 46.

[*Phot. F. Bruckmann A.G., Munich*]

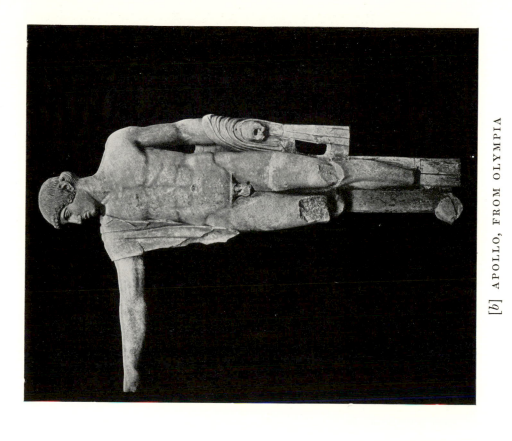

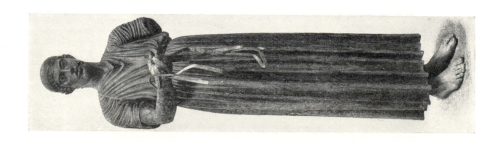

[*a*] Apollo; in the *British Museum*. Roman copy in marble of a bronze of about 470 B.C. The nose is modern. (v, 427.)

[*Brit. Mus. Marbles and Bronzes*, Pl. III]

[*b*] Fragmentary marble woman: from the Acropolis of Athens; in *Athens* (Acropolis no. 688). About 470 B.C. (v, 427.)

[H. Schrader, *Auswahl arch. Marmor. Sculpt. im Akrop. Mus.*, fig. 40]

[*c*] Apollo; in *Cassel*. Roman copy in marble of a bronze of about 460 B.C. He probably held bow and laurel-wreath. (v, 427.)

[M. Bieber, *Die Antike Skulpt. d. kgl. Mus. in Cassel*, Pl. III]

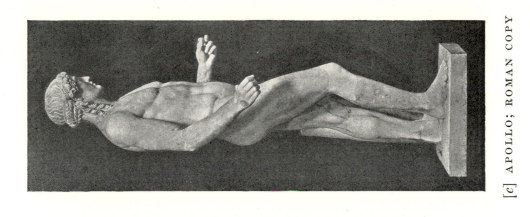

[b] FRAGMENTARY STATUE
FROM THE ACROPOLIS
OF ATHENS

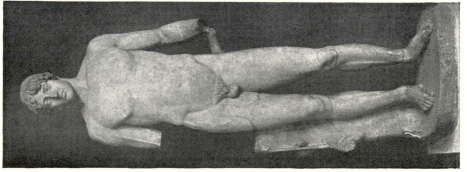

[a] APOLLO; ROMAN COPY

[a] Goddess (the so-called Hestia Giustiniani); in the *Torlonia Collection* at *Rome*. Roman copy in marble of a bronze of about 460 B.C. The feet and the sceptre are missing: part of the nose is modern. Photograph from a cast. (v, 428, 441; vi, 539.)

[b] Harmodius; in *Naples*. Part of a Roman copy in marble of the bronze group of the Tyrant-slayers, by Critius and Nesiotes, which was set up in Athens in 476 B.C. Photograph from a cast. Above; shield of Athena on a panathenaic amphora; in the *British Museum* (B. 605). The device is the Tyrant-slayers after the group by Critius and Nesiotes. (iv, 80; v, 428; vi, 539.)

[c] The statue called 'Amelung's.' Roman copy of a bronze goddess of about 460 B.C. The cast from which the photograph is taken is composed of a head in *Berlin* and a body in *Berlin*. (v, 428.)

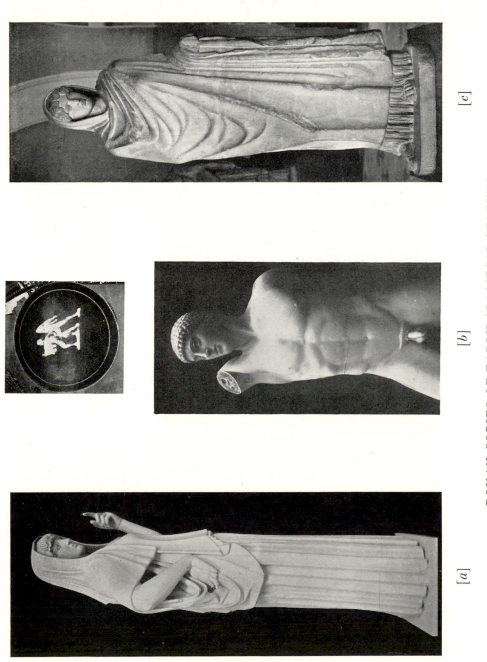

[a]

[b]

[c]

ROMAN COPIES OF EARLY CLASSICAL STATUES

MYRON

[*a*] Discus-thrower: copy of a bronze by Myron, about 450 B.C. The photograph is taken from a restored cast which combines a body in the *Terme Museum* in *Rome* and a head in the *Lancellotti Collection, Rome*. (v, 429.)

[*Phot. F. Bruckmann A.G., Munich*]

[*b*], [*c*] The original bronze group depicting Athena and Marsyas stood in Athens. Athena has dropped the flute and turned to pass on; the satyr, who has been listening awe-struck, steals up after the discarded flute, while the goddess looks round with a warning gesture, for the flute will be his death. These are Roman marble copies: the Athena in *Frankfort*, the Marsyas in the *Lateran* at *Rome*. Photographs from casts. (v, 429.)

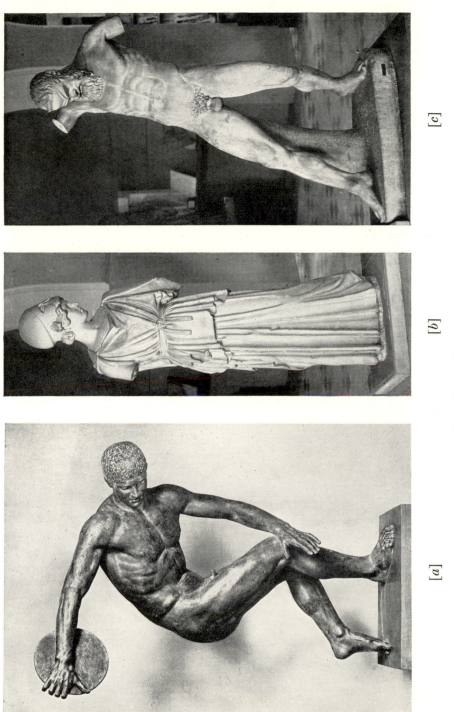

[a]　　　　[b]　　　　[c]

COPIES OF STATUES BY MYRON

THE TEMPLE OF ZEUS AT OLYMPIA

[a], [b] Figures from the east pediment of the Temple: [a] a seer;
[b] a youth watching.

[c] A lapith boy struggling with a centaur from the west pediment.
In *Olympia*. About 460 B.C. (v, 430 *sqq.*)

[Buschor and Hamann, *Die Skulpt. des Zeustempels in Olympia*]

[c]

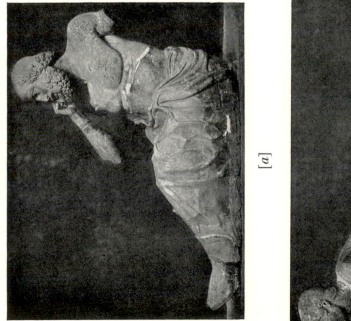

[a]

[b]

STATUES FROM THE TEMPLE OF ZEUS AT OLYMPIA

EARLY CLASSICAL SCULPTURE

THE TEMPLE OF ZEUS AT OLYMPIA; METOPES

[*a*] Heracles offering the dead bodies of the Stymphalian birds to Athena.

[*b*] Heracles supporting the firmament, Athena lends him a hand, Atlas fetches him the golden apples. In *Olympia*. About 460 B.C. (v, 430.)

[Buschor and Hamann, *l.c.*]

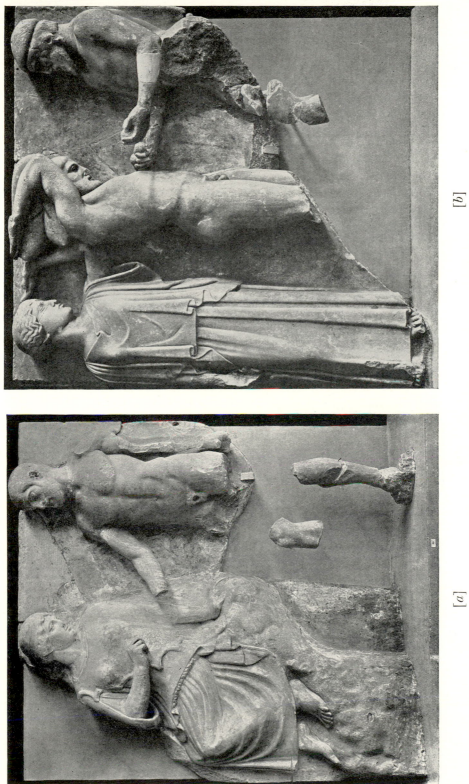

[a]   [b]

METOPES OF THE TEMPLE OF ZEUS AT OLYMPIA

[*a*] Heracles rallying the Argonauts at Lemnos: from a calyx-krater by the Niobid painter; in the *Louvre, Paris*. About 460–450 B.C. (v, 432.)

[*Furtwängler and Reichhold*, Pl. 108; F. Bruckmann A.G., Munich]

[*b*] Calyx-krater; in *Bologna*. Amazonomachy. About 460–450 B.C. (v, 434.)

[*Phot. Alinari*]

[a] FROM A CALYX-KRATER BY THE NIOBID PAINTER

[b] CALYX-KRATER, IN BOLOGNA

[*a*] Achilles and Penthesilea: from a drinking-cup by the Penthesilea painter; in *Munich*. About 470–460 B.C. (v, 434.)

[*Furtwängler and Reichhold*, Pl. 75; F. Bruckmann A.G., Munich]

[*b*] Aphrodite: from a white drinking-cup by the Pistoxenus painter; in the *British Museum* (D. 2). About 460 B.C. (v, 434.)

[a] DRINKING-CUP BY THE PENTHESILEA PAINTER

[b] DRINKING-CUP BY THE PISTOXENUS PAINTER

[a], [b] Two small white drinking-cups by the Sotades painter; in the *British Museum*. On the first Hippomedon attacks the serpent which has killed the infant Archemorus; a fragment on the left of the cup shows that the nurse Hypsipyle appeared in the picture. The second cup shows a girl standing on tip-toe picking apples from a tree. About 470 B.C. (v, 434.)

[a]

[b]

DRINKING-CUPS BY THE SOTADES PAINTER

POLYCLITUS

[a] Athlete with a spear: from *Pompeii*; in *Naples*. Roman copy, in marble, of the bronze 'doryphorus' by Polyclitus. The spear is modern. (v, 435 *sq.*)

[*Phot. Brogi*]

[b] Athlete (or Apollo?) binding his head with the victor's fillet. Marble copy found in *Delos*, made in the second century B.C., of a bronze by Polyclitus. In *Athens*. (v, 436.)

[*Phot. Alinari*]

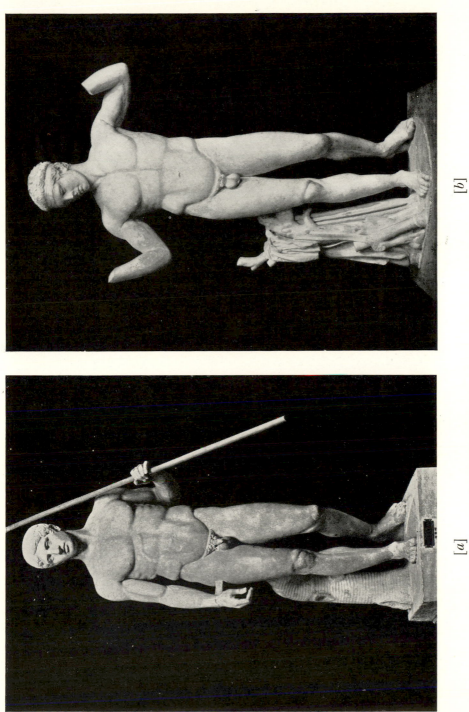

[a]

[b]

COPIES OF POLYCLEITAN STATUES

[*a*] Amazon; in *Berlin*: Roman copy, in marble, after a bronze of
about 430 B.C. (v, 436.)

[*Phot. Berlin Museum*]

[*b*] Amazon; in the *Capitoline Museum* at *Rome*. Roman copy, in
marble, after a bronze of about 430 B.C., probably by Polyclitus.
(v, 436.)

[*Phot. Berlin Museum*]

[*c*] Boy athlete: from Egypt; in the *Louvre, Paris*. Roman copy,
in marble, of a bronze by a follower of Polyclitus. (v, 437.)

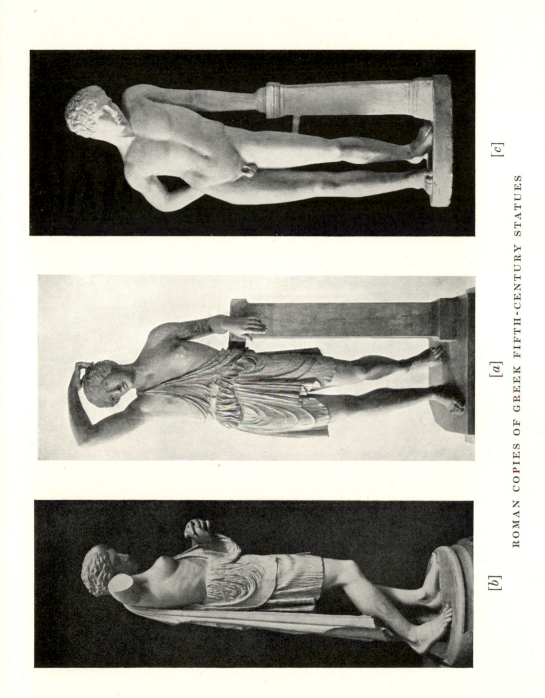

[b]　　　　　　[a]　　　　　　[c]

ROMAN COPIES OF GREEK FIFTH-CENTURY STATUES

[*a*]   Goddess; in *Cherchel*. Roman copy of an original of about
440 B.C. Marble. (v, 441.)

[Kekulé, *Frauenstatue aus der Zeit des Phidias* (1897)]

[*b*]   A marble boy: from *Rhamnus*; in *Athens*. From a cast. (v, 438.)

[*c*]   Small marble head, probably of Zeus; in *Copenhagen*. (v, 437.)

[*Phot. Giraudon*]

[b] BOY, FROM RHAMNUS

[a] GODDESS, IN CHERCHEL

[c] HEAD, IN COPENHAGEN

THE PARTHENON

[*a*] One of the metopes, still in position on the south side of the building. A centaur and lapith.

[*b*], [*c*] From the frieze: horsemen preparing to mount and riding in the procession; [*b*] *in situ* at *Athens* (from a cast); [*c*] in the *British Museum*. (v, 439, 440.)

[A. H. Smith, *The Sculptures of the Parthenon*, Pls. 16, 61, 71]

[a]

[b]

[c]

SCULPTURES FROM THE PARTHENON

THE PARTHENON

[a] A back-view of the reclining figure variously described as Theseus or Dionysus, from the east pediment. From a cast.

[*Phot. Berlin Museum*]

[b] The Three Fates from the same pediment. (v, 440.)

[A. H. Smith, *l.c.*]

[a]

[b]

SCULPTURES FROM THE PARTHENON

[*a*] Amazonomachy: from the frieze of the Temple of Apollo at
Phigalea; about 420 B.C.; in the *British Museum*. (v, 442.)

[*Photograph by Mr Ashmole*]

[*b*] Attic tombstone of the later part of the fifth century B.C.; in
Athens. (v, 442.)

[*Phot. Alinari*]

[a] PART OF THE FRIEZE OF THE TEMPLE AT PHIGALEA

[b] ATTIC TOMBSTONE

CLASSICAL SCULPTURE: SECOND HALF OF THE FIFTH CENTURY

[a] Bronze boy, from *Pompeii*; in *Naples*: Roman copy of a work of about 440 B.C. The right hand held something now lost. (v, 442.)

[*Phot. Alinari*]

[b] Athlete; in *New York*: marble copy of a bronze of about 440–430 B.C. (v, 442.)

[*Phot. Metropolitan Mus., New York*]

[c] Bronze boy victor, from *Pesaro*; in *Florence*. About 440–430 B.C. (v, 442.)

[*Phot. Alinari*]

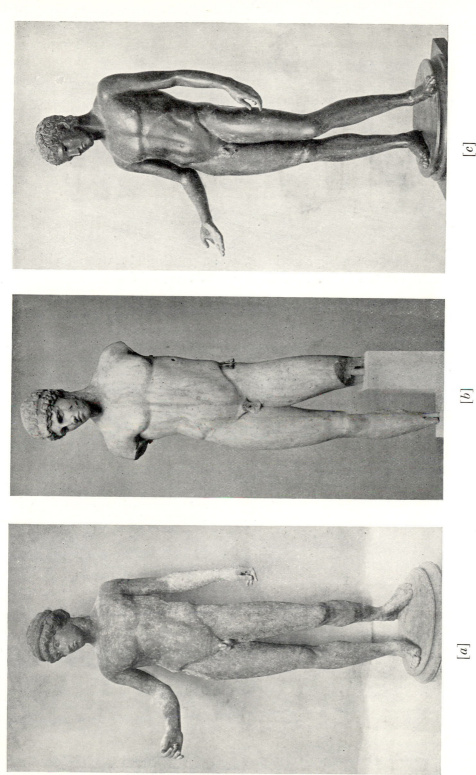

[a]

[b]

[c]

[*a*] From a white lekythos in *Athens*: a youth and a woman with offerings at the tomb. About 440–430 B.C. (v, 443.)

[W. Riezler, *Weissgrundige attische Lekythen*, Pl. 23]

[*b*] Two white lekythoi, in *Munich*: on one, two women at the tomb: on the other Hermes, and a woman making ready for the grave. About 430 B.C. (v, 443.)

[E. Buschor, *Attische Lekythen der Parthenonzeit*, Pl. 1; *Münchener Jahrb. d. bild. Kunst, Neue Folge*; G. D. W. Callwey, Munich]

[a]

[b]

ATTIC WHITE LEKYTHOI

[*a*] Maenads dancing: from a volute-krater, by the painter of the
Berlin dinos; in *Bologna*. About 420 B.C. (v, 444.)

[*Photograph by Mrs Beazley*]

[*b*] The rape of the daughters of Leucippus: detail from a hydria
by the Meidias painter; in the *British Museum*. End of the fifth
century B.C. (v, 444.)

[*Furtwängler and Reichhold*, Pl. 8; F. Brückmann A.G., Munich]

[*c*] The dead warrior, with a woman and a youth: from a white
lekythos; in *Athens*. About 400 B.C. (v, 444.)

[W. Riezler, *Weissgrundige at'ische Lekythen*, Pl. 90]

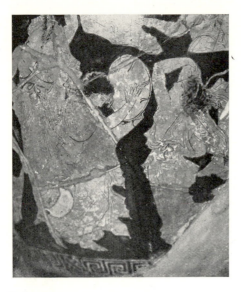

[a] FROM A KRATER BY THE
PAINTER OF THE BERLIN DINOS

[b] FROM A HYDRIA BY THE
MEIDIAS PAINTER

[c] FROM A WHITE LEKYTHOS

ARCHITECTURE: THE FIFTH CENTURY

[*a*] The later HEXASTYLE DORIC TEMPLE at *Posidonia* (after-
wards called *Paestum*), known as the 'Temple of Poseidon,' built
in the fifth century B.C., perhaps in its first half. The photograph is
taken from the east porch, just outside the threshold of the main
door, and shows the two rows of inner columns, with some of the
smaller upper columns and their architraves still in position. Much
of the cella walls has been removed or destroyed: the columns and
superstructure of the northern outer colonnade (or pteron), of the
west porch, and of the west pteron, partly seen in the photograph,
were all originally invisible from this point. (v, 446.)

[*Phot. Hellenic Society*]

[*b*] The west end of the PARTHENON at *Athens*, built, in its surviving form, by Ictinus and Callicrates, and begun in 447 B.C. This
pediment contains the only important statues still in place. The
explosion of 1687 A.D. blew out the middle of the temple, and the
isolated columns here shown have been set up again in modern
times: further restoration is now being carried out. The arch visible
between the columns is Byzantine. Under the three marble steps
can be seen the top of the older limestone substructure, which the
builders of the surviving temple completely buried. (v, 448. For
plan of the temple see no. 5, facing p. 464: for some of the sculptures
see pp. 60, 62 above.)

[*Photograph by Mr M. Ziffo*]

[a] TEMPLE AT POSIDONIA

[b] THE PARTHENON

[a] The PROPYLAEA at *Athens*, designed by Mnesicles, begun in 437 B.C., seen from the south-west. The photograph shows the north-west hall and part of the hexastyle Doric façade of the west porch, with the gap for the carriage-road between its central columns. Besides the obvious loss of all the roofing, much of the entablature, and parts of the Doric columns, the Ionic columns inside the west porch have fallen: they would have been partly visible from this point. (v, 451. For plan of the building see no. 3, facing p. 464.)

[*Photograph by Mr M. Ziffo*]

[b] The north-east Ionic column, inside the west porch of the PROPYLAEA, seen from below, and from the south-west. This column, with part of the marble ceiling, which originally covered the whole porch, has been thus re-erected in modern times. The upper part of one of the doors by which pedestrians passed through the wall separating the west and east porches can be seen, and through it one of the Doric columns of the east porch, black against the sky. (v, 450.)

[*Photograph by Mr L. P. Thompson*]

[c] The interior of the west porch of the PROPYLAEA, from the north-east, showing half one of its fallen Ionic capitals, badly damaged, placed upside down on the bottom drum of the fallen north-west Ionic column. The abacus of the capital has lost its egg-and-tongue carving. The rebuilt temple of Athena Nike, on its bastion, is partly visible through the Doric columns of the west façade. (v, 451.)

[*Phot. Hellenic Society*]

74

[a]

[b]

[c]

THE PROPYLAEA AT ATHENS

[a] The ERECHTHEUM at *Athens*, perhaps begun about 421 B.C., seen from the south-west. The lower part of the central portion is hidden by the ruins of the substructure of the old temple of Athena Polias, the top of which is roughly level with the Maiden Porch, visible to the right, and with the East Porch. The North Porch has lost its pediment, and all the roofing has disappeared: the frieze has lost its reliefs, which consisted of white marble figures applied to a background of black limestone. The central portion, with engaged columns and windows, is a Roman restoration, and there has been much judicious modern reconstruction. (v, 454. For plan of the temple see no. 4, facing p. 464.)

[*Photograph by Mr M. Ziffo*]

[b] The Maiden Porch of the ERECHTHEUM, from the south-east, partly restored, and strengthened with metal bars. The caryatid second from the left is in the British Museum: the figure seen in the photograph is a terra-cotta reproduction. The gap behind the pedestal at the north-east corner led to the staircase which descended into the interior. It can be seen that this Porch, unlike the other two, has dentils, but no frieze. (v, 454.)

[*Photograph by Mr M. Ziffo*]

[a]

[b]

THE ERECHTHEUM AT ATHENS

ARCHITECTURE: THE FIFTH CENTURY

[*a*] The interior of the HEXASTYLE DORIC TEMPLE OF APOLLO at *Bassae* near *Phigalea* in Arcadia, built in the second half of the fifth century B.C. The photograph is taken from the inner part of the cella, looking north, and out through the north door and the north porch. The base of the single Corinthian column stands in the foreground, and some of the tongue-walls, with their engaged Ionic columns, partly rebuilt, are visible on each side. The curious spreading bases are still in position, but the capitals have perished, except for fragments, though some found complete were drawn in the early nineteenth century. These half-columns carried an architrave and a frieze, which is now in the British Museum. (v, 456. For plan of the temple see no. 5, facing p. 464: for part of the frieze of the temple see p. 64 [*a*].)

[*Photograph by Mr L. P. Thompson*]

[*b*] The same temple. The photograph is taken from the south-west corner of the outer part of the cella, looking north-west across the inner part of the cella and out of the east side-door, opposite which probably stood the god's statue. The base of the Corinthian column and one of the two southernmost tongue-walls, which projected at an angle of 45 degrees, are visible in the foreground. (v, 456.)

[*Photograph by Mr L. P. Thompson*]

[*c*] Haller von Hallerstein's drawing of the lost capital of the Corinthian column of the same temple, made soon after its discovery: the outer spirals had been destroyed before it was found. This is the earliest known Corinthian capital: notable features are the lowness and unusual form of the ring of acanthus leaves, the large size of the inner spirals, the palmette on the bell (which was originally taller), the absence of a sheath common to the outer and inner spirals, the heaviness of the abacus, and the painted decoration on the abacus and on the bell. (v, 457.)

[*Phot. deutsch. Archäol. Institut*]

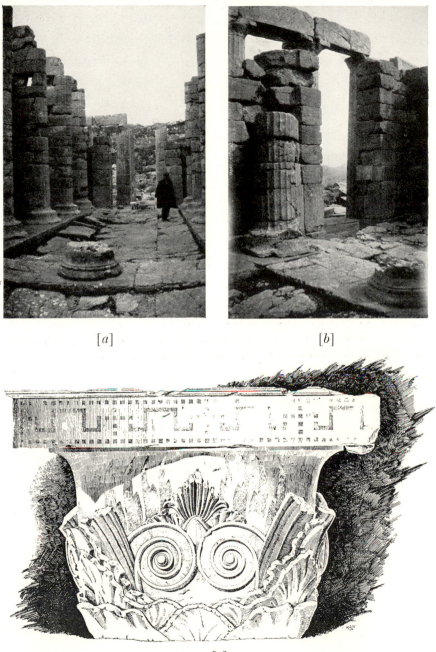

[a]

[b]

[c]

THE TEMPLE OF APOLLO AT BASSAE

[*a*] Eirene and Plutus—Peace with the infant Wealth in her arms—
in *Munich*: Roman copy, in marble, of a bronze by Cephisodotus,
set up at Athens shortly after 375 B.C. The photograph is from
a cast. (vi, 77, 539.)

[*b*] Athena in *Florence*: Roman copy, in marble, of a bronze be-
longing to the earlier part of the fourth century B.C. The spear, most
of the right arm and the nose, are modern. (vi, 359.)

[*Phot. Alinari*]

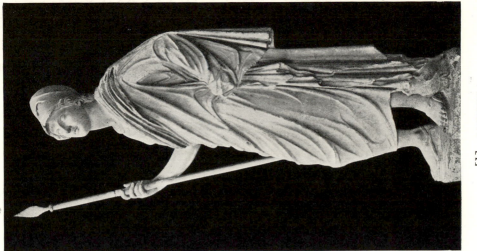

[b] ATHENA

[a] EIRENE

PRAXITELES

[a], [b] Hermes with the infant Dionysus, by Praxiteles; in *Olympia*. [a] From the original, [b] from a cast. Modern, the legs from below the knee, except the right foot. (vi, 536 *sq.*)

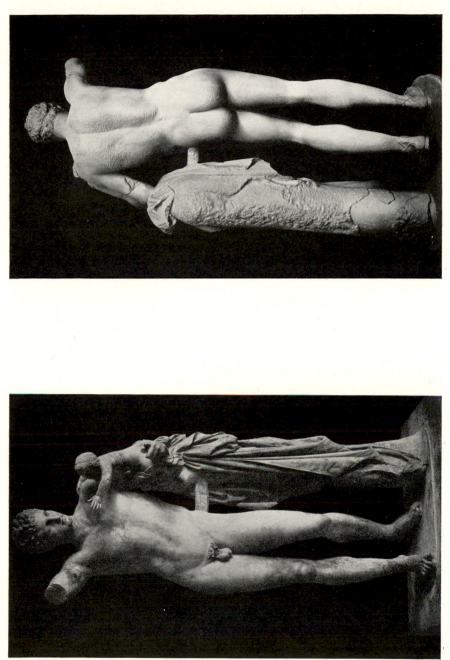

[a]

[b]

THE HERMES OF PRAXITELES

SCOPAS

[a] Fragment of a Tritoness, from Ostia; in *Ostia*. Copy or imitation of one of the figures in a group of Poseidon, demigods and monsters of the deep made by Scopas. From a cast. (vi, 538.)

[b] Maenad; in *Dresden*. Fragment of a reduced copy of the Maenad by Scopas. (vi, 537 *sq*.)

[*Phot. Dresden Mus.*]

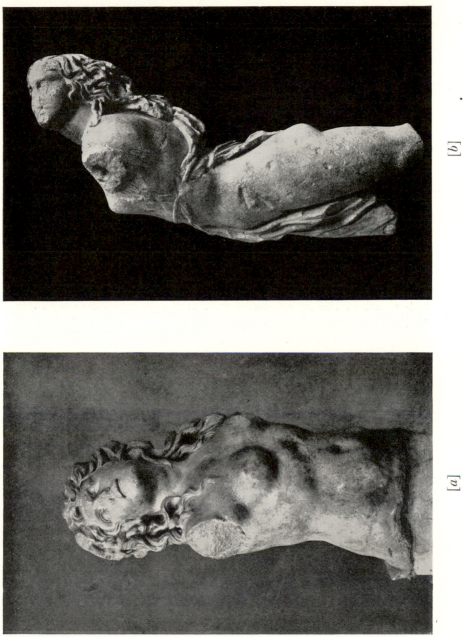

[*a*], [*b*] Two fragmentary heads, one of Heracles the other of a young warrior, from the west pediment of the temple of Athena Alea at *Tegea* (see p. 112); in *Athens*. Scopas was the architect and the sculpture must be of his school and from his designs. From casts. (vi, 538.)

[*Photographs by Dr K. Neugebauer*]

[*c*] Head of girl goddess (part of a statue) from *Chios*; in *Boston*. Later part of the fourth century B.C.: manner of Praxiteles. (vi, 540.)

[*d*] Head of a goddess (part of a statue) from *Athens*; in *Boston*. Later part of the fourth century B.C.: manner of Praxiteles. (vi, 540.)

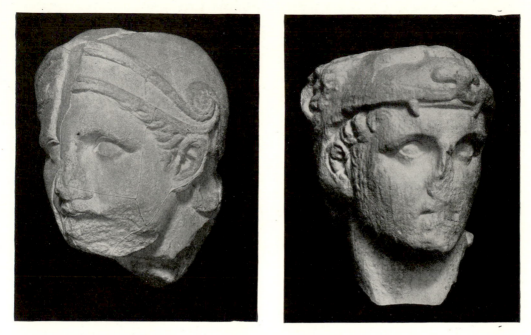

[a]   [b]

HEADS FROM THE TEMPLE OF ATHENA ALEA AT TEGEA

[c]   [d]

HEADS OF GODDESSES

[*a*] Hypnos, the god of Sleep: marble copy in *Madrid*, from a bronze; later part of the fourth century B.C. Photograph from a cast. (vi, 538.)

[*b*] Demeter, from *Cnidus*; in the *British Museum*. (vi, 539.)

[*Phot. British Museum*]

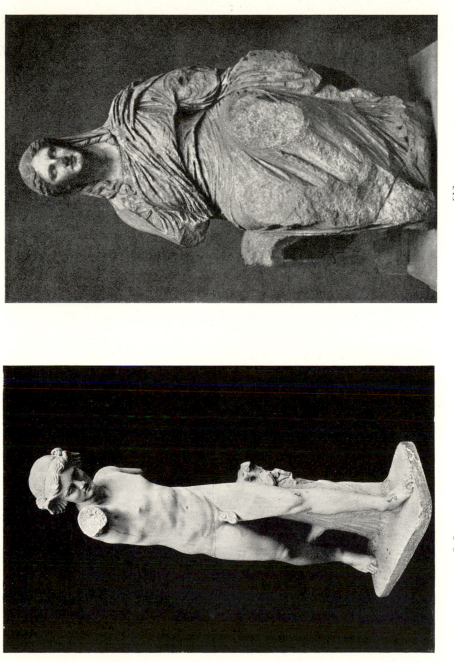

[a] HYPNOS

[b] DEMETER

[a], [b] Two slabs from the tomb of Mausolus at *Halicarnassus*; in the *British Museum*. Amazonomachy. Middle of the fourth century B.C. (vi, 540 *sq.*)

[c] Part of another work done by a Greek for a foreigner. One side of the so-called Alexander sarcophagus in *Constantinople* found at *Sidon*. (See also p. 92 [a], [b].) (vi, 541.)

[Hamdy Bey and Reinach, *Nécropole Royale à Sidon*, Pl. 30.]

)

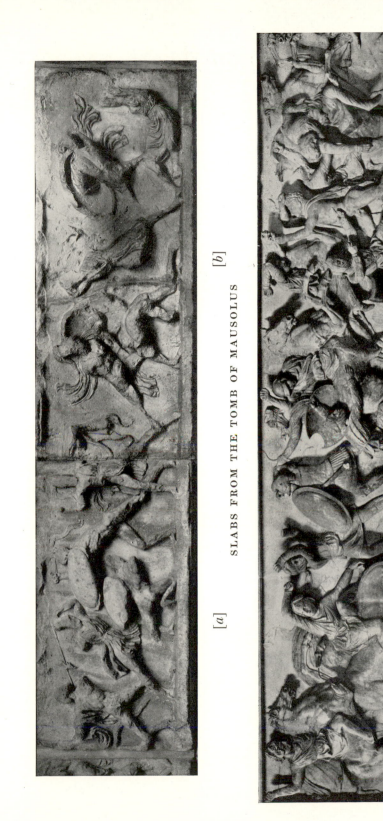

[a]

[b]

SLABS FROM THE TOMB OF MAUSOLUS

[c]

PART OF THE ALEXANDER SARCOPHAGUS, FROM SIDON

[a], [b] Heads from the Alexander sarcophagus from *Sidon* (p. 90 [c]). [b] is Alexander, wearing the lion's scalp (see p. 90 [b]). End of the fourth century B.C. (vi, 541.)

[c] Head of the statue of the athlete Agias, from *Delphi*; in *Delphi*. (See p. 94 [b] and p. 96 [a].) About 340 B.C. (vi, 542.)

[b] HEAD FROM THE ALEXANDER SARCOPHAGUS, FROM SIDON

[c] HEAD OF AGIAS

[a] HEAD FROM THE ALEXANDER SARCOPHAGUS, FROM SIDON

LYSIPPUS

[a] Athlete scraping himself with a strigil; in the *Vatican*. A marble copy of a bronze by Lysippus. The end of the nose is modern. Photograph from a cast. (vi, 541.)

[b] The athlete Agias, from *Delphi*; in *Delphi*. A fourth-century marble, perhaps a copy of a bronze by Lysippus. The ankles are modern. Photograph from a cast. (See p. 92 [c] and p. 96 [a].) (vi, 542.)

[a] ATHLETE

[b] AGIAS

LYSIPPUS

[a] Agias (p. 94 [b]). (vi, 542.)

[*Fouilles de Delphes*, iv, Pl. 63]

[b] Silenus with the infant Dionysus: a marble copy in the *Louvre, Paris,* of a bronze of the school of Lysippus. Modern, the hands of Silenus, the hands and arms of the child. (vi, 542.)

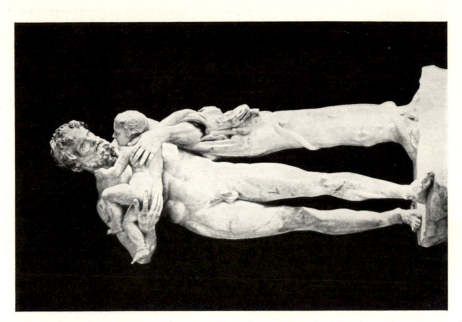

[b] SILENUS

[a] AGIAS

[a] Athlete, loosening his sandals, in *Lansdowne House*. The right hand modern. Copy of a bronze in the manner of Lysippus. Photograph from a cast. (vi, 542.)

[b] Bronze statue of a boy from the sea near *Marathon*; in *Athens*. The motive of the arms is not yet explained. Late fourth century B.C.

[*Phot. Alinari*]

[b] BRONZE BOY

[a] ATHLETE, LOOSENING HIS SANDALS

7-2

[*a*] Marble statuette of Artemis, from *Larnaca* in *Cyprus*; in *Vienna*. Late fourth century B.C. School of Praxiteles. (vi, 540.)

[*b*] Marble statuette of Socrates, from *Egypt*; in the *British Museum*: reduced copy of a fourth-century original. (vi, 543.)

ATTIC TOMBSTONES

[a] Tombstone of Sostrate in the *Metropolitan Museum, New York*; showing the survival of fifth-century tradition, with only the beginning of change. (vi, 544.)

[*Phot. Metropolitan Museum*]

[b] Tombstone from Athens; in *Athens* (no. 870): full fourth-century style. (vi, 544.)

[*Phot. Alinari*]

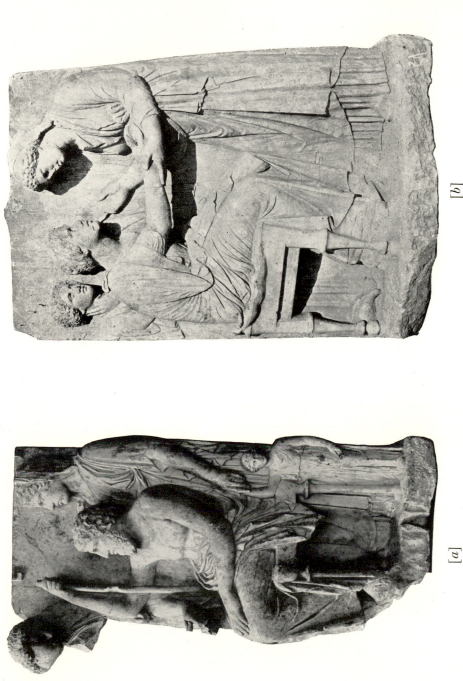

[a]

[b]

ATTIC TOMBSTONES

ATTIC TOMBSTONES

[a] Tombstone from the *Ilissus*; in *Athens*. Second half of the fourth century B.C. (vi, 544.)

[b] Tombstone in *Athens* (no. 731). Later part of the fourth century B.C. (vi, 544.)

[*Phots. Alinari*]

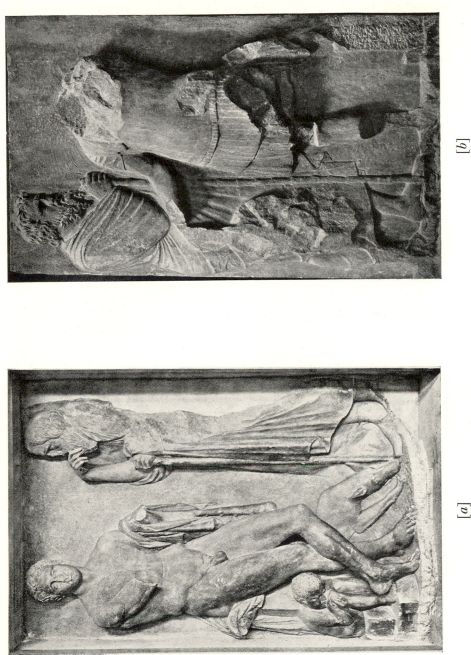

[b]

[a]

ATTIC TOMBSTONES

[a] From a calyx-krater, found at *Pisticci*; in the *British Museum*: Dolon caught by Diomede and Odysseus: a burlesque of an epic scene. Italiote work of about 400 B.C. (vi, 545.)

[*Furtwängler and Reichhold*, Pl. 110, 4 *a*; F. Brückmann A.G., Munich]

[b] Calyx-krater in *Harvard*. Aphrodite and Silens. Attic, second half of the fourth century B.C. (vi, 545.)

[c] Fragment of a bell-krater in *Heidelberg*, depicting a scene from a farce—an old gentleman and a parasite. Part of the parasite's leg is modern. Italiote work of the beginning of the fourth century B.C. (vi, 545.)

[a] ODYSSEUS, DOLON AND DIOMEDE, FROM A CALYX-KRATER

[c] FRAGMENT OF A BELL-KRATER

[b] CALYX-KRATER: APHRODITE
AND SILENS

[*a*] Aphrodite and Eros: engraved on a bronze mirror-cover; in the *Louvre, Paris* (de Ridder, *Cat. Bronzes Antiq. du Louvre*, no. 1700). The style is like that of Attic vases in the second half of the fourth century B.C. (vi, 545.)

[*Phot. Giraudon*]

[*b*] Part of an ivory lyre, engraved and coloured, from *Kerch* (ancient Panticapaeum); in *Leningrad*. The subject was the Judgement of Paris: this piece gives Aphrodite and Athena. The style is like that of the mirror-cover [*a*] above. (vi, 545.)

[E. H. Minns, *Scythians and Greeks*, p. 204 B]

[*a*] BRONZE MIRROR-COVER

[*b*] FRAGMENT OF AN IVORY LYRE

Mosaic from *Pompeii*; in *Naples*. A copy, fragmentary and damaged, of a fourth-century picture by Philoxenus of Eretria: the meeting of Alexander and Darius. (v, 433; vi, 545 *sq*.)

[*Phot. Alinari*]

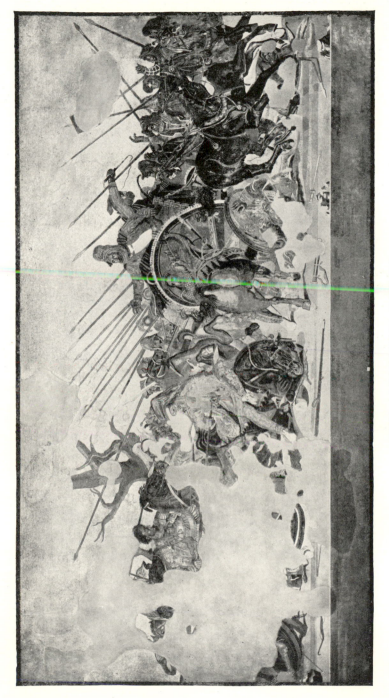

THE ALEXANDER MOSAIC

Restoration of the east front of the Doric TEMPLE OF ATHENA ALEA at *Tegea*, in *Arcadia*: built of local marble in the first half of the fourth century B.C. The architect was the sculptor Scopas. The slender column-shaft and low straight echinus are typical of the period: the temple of Zeus at Nemea, perhaps a later work of the same architect, carries these tendencies even further. The Tegean temple had pedimental sculpture, not shown in the illustration, but of the metopes only those over the cella porches, inside the colonnade, were carved. The outer faces of the side-walls of the cella are in line with the axes of the penultimate columns of the façades: this is the classical practice in peripteral Doric temples, but in Ionic the axes of the cella walls usually coincide with those of these columns. (vi, 547, 550; plan of the temple, vi, opposite p. 558; Corinthian capital from interior on the next plate, p. 114 [*a*]; heads of statues from the pediment on p. 86 [*a*], [*b*] above.)

[C. Dugas *Le Sanctuaire d'Aléa Athéna à Tegéa au IVe siècle*, 1924, Pls. XII–XIV]

RESTORATION OF EAST FRONT OF TEMPLE OF
ATHENA ALEA AT TEGEA

[*a*] Engaged marble CORINTHIAN CAPITAL from the half-columns inside the Doric TEMPLE OF ATHENA ALEA at *Tegea*, reconstructed from fragments. These capitals are low and squat: they show what is probably the earliest example of the fluted *cauliculus* sheathing the angle spirals, a feature which later became orthodox, but a single tall acanthus leaf replaces the inner spirals and central ornament. (vi, 548, 550; plan of the temple, vi, opposite p. 558: restoration of façade on the preceding plate, p. 112.)

[*L.c.*, Pl. LXXVI]

[*b*] Marble CORINTHIAN CAPITAL designed for one of the inner columns of the circular *tholos* at *Epidaurus*, built by the sculptor Polyclitus the younger, probably between 360 and 330 B.C. This specimen, for unknown reasons, was buried unused, and is therefore wonderfully perfect. The design is light and delicate: the outer and inner spirals are independent, and do not spring from a sheath: above the inner spirals a flower takes the place of the palmette used in the earlier Corinthian capital of Bassae, illustrated on p. 78 [*c*] above. (vi, 549, 551; plan of the *tholos*, vi, opposite p. 558.)

[*Phot. Hellenic Society*]

[a] CAPITAL FROM TEMPLE OF ATHENA ALEA AT TEGEA

[b] CAPITAL DESIGNED FOR THE THOLOS AT EPIDAURUS

8-2

[a] Front and under views of the Corinthian capital of one of the engaged stone columns inside the circular Philippeum at *Olympia*, probably built by Alexander the Great. Both in general proportion and in detail these capitals on the whole anticipate later orthodoxy more nearly than do any of their predecessors, but the inner spirals and central ornament are omitted, as at Tegea, being replaced by a series of narrow upright leaves. (vi, 552.)

[*Olympia, Ergebnisse, Die Baudenkmäler*, Pl. LXXXI]

[b] Reconstructed cast at Berlin of upper part of one column and part of the side entablature from the marble Ionic temple of ATHENA POLIAS at *Priene*, dedicated by Alexander the Great: the triply-fasciated architrave, large dentils, and sima-crowned cornice are separated by egg-and-tongue ornament resting on bead-and-reel: the absence of a frieze between architrave and dentils has been disputed, but is almost certain. A. v. Gerkan has shown in *Ath. Mitt.*, xliii, 1918, p. 165, that the dentils should be set a little farther back. In the capital, the eye of the volute is at once well outside the perpendicular of the upper diameter of the column-shaft and well above the horizontal of the bottom of the echinus. The sima is a genuine gutter, pierced with lion-head spouts. (vi, 554; plan of the temple, 3 opposite vi, p. 558.)

[Wiegand and Schrader, *Priene*, 1904, p. 102, fig. 71]

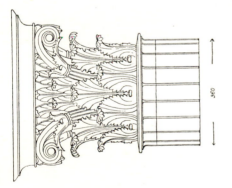

[*a*] Head of a statue of a woman, wearing a short wig: life-size. Black granite. Early Ptolemaic period; third century B.C. *Brit. Mus.* no. 57355; height 26·6 cm.

[*b*], [*c*] Late Saïte portrait statues: granite and limestone: XXVIIIth Dynasty. Sixth century B.C. The 'archaic smile,' borrowed from early Greek art, is well seen in [*c*]. *Brit. Mus.* nos. 1646, 37894; [*b*] height 1 metre 6·8 cm., [*c*] height 57·2 cm.

[*d*] Ptolemaic squatting figure: granite. Shows the degeneration of the Saïte type in a dry conventional style. Third–second century B.C. *Brit. Mus.* no. 54348; height 45·7 cm. (vi, 159 *sqq.*)

[a] EARLY PTOLEMAIC PORTRAIT

[b]   [c]   [d]

LATE SAÏTE AND PTOLEMAIC FIGURES

[a] Black steatite bowl, fourth century B.C., with procession in relief of musicians and dancers. A remarkable example of the graecizing style of the period immediately preceding and contemporary with the Macedonian conquest, exemplified on a larger scale in the Tomb of Petosiris at Deruah, published by Lefebvre, *Le Tombeau de Petrosis*, 1924–5. *Brit. Mus.* no. 47992; height 7 cm., diam. 12·3 cm.

[b] Blue faience bowl, fourth century B.C., with relief-bands of animals and birds round a central rosette. A very fine example of the same period, in faience. Fourth century B.C. *Brit. Mus.* no. 57385; height 5·7 cm., diam. 13 cm.

[a] STEATITE BOWL

[b] FAIENCE BOWL